LVSE.

E.J. Tiago

LVSE.

FiveOneEight Publishing, 2021, Illinois.

Copyright © 2021 E.J. Tiago.

All rights reserved.

ISBN: 9798772612040

Dedication

This is dedicated to anyone who has fallen in love and doesn't believe they will again.

You will.

E.J. Tiago

LVSE.

<u>Molly pt.1</u>

I've never been a morning person.
It's such an awful concept.
Hours of silence and darkness
followed by loud noises and bright lights.
But my favorite part of the morning
is looking in the mirror.

Something about my reflection
makes me feel at ease,
…at peace.

When I smile,
you smile.
When you laugh,
I laugh.
When I say I love you,
you say you love me too.

LVSE.

> Flaws and all,
> I see the best parts of me,
> through you.

> Whenever I see your happiness,
> it feels as if I'm looking in the mirror.

LVSE.

Wow

Every time I walk in a room,
you smile…
And immediately,
I feel loved.

Beautiful poem

Her hands grab my attention,
as they reach for red wine.
Noticing newly painted red nails,
I imagine how my penis
would replace the glass.

As she lays in my bed naked,
I stare at lips I kissed seconds ago.
When she starts to talk,
I think of how I was inside your mouth.
It makes every word she says,
Beautiful to me.

LVSE.

<u>Colombia</u>

You come to mind,
from time to time.

My aim isn't to miss you,
but kiss you.
Because I am not ready to be forgotten.

LVSE.

Lo vi

I saw you two hours ago,
and it feels like two days have passed.
I want to ask,

When can I see you again,
when can I breathe you again,
when can I be near you again.

I have to remind myself,
It's only been two hours since I seen you last.
Regardless… if 7,200 seconds have passed.

I don't know what tomorrow holds,
but from experience,
it never has a good grip on today.

And today,
I want to know when our next tomorrow is.

LVSE.

<u>Did you</u>

When we went home together that night,
what thoughts ran through your mind?
Did you think about us?
Did you think about love?

Did you look at my appearance
with more attention to the details?
Did you glimpse into my eyes
to remember the color?
Did you think,
this could be the last waterfall
our bare skins would experience…
together.

Did you stare at my physique,
or take a sneak peak
to memorize my features?
Did you get tired since you knew
this is the last time we'd lay together.
That this would be the last goodnight kiss I
laid on your forehead.

LVSE.

Did you kiss me to learn how my lips would feel?
Did you hold me
incase this was the last time
you'd feel my hands grips your waist as you climax.

For love,
I spent all night knowing it could be,
So yes,
I did exactly just that..

LVSE.

Love is

Love is when we first met.
Love is what I can't forget.

Love is knowing we aren't together.
Love is hoping you are somewhere better.

Love is the fact,
a part of my heart
will always love
that person I met.
And I accept.

LVSE.

<u>Babe</u>

Without you, I sleep like a baby.

I wake up every hour,
crying,
wondering,
where you are…
and why you aren't holding me.

LVSE.

<u>Regrats</u>

I'm not America's top chef,
but in the running for America's top regrets.
I've made mistakes the country would salivate
over.

Regrets to me is a mother's unconditional love.
Not matter how much I try
and push them away,
they will always stay.

Regardless of all my bad decisions,
loving you was never one of them.

LVSE.

<u>Vowels</u>

a, e, i, o, u.

They may seem like just vowels,
but hey,
every word needs a vowel…
at least one.

The more I think about it,
the more it makes sense.
I am the word that needs

You.

LVSE.

<u>Lighters</u>

She looks at him with an affectionate glare.
The same way she looks at fireworks
during a perfect night of flare.
No words need to be said.
Just twinkling eyes
and sign language through her dimples.

LVSE.

<u>NYC</u>

As I walk along the streets of NYC,
looking for where to go and what to see.
He grabs my arm,
to hold my hand.
I'm instantly brought back to reality.

I know we'll never get lost
since you have been found.

LVSE.

__What a waste__

Thank you for wasting my time,
all of it.
All of it was a waste.

The days laced in laughter.
Our afternoon adventures.
The never-ending nights.
The missteps made.
The artful arguments.
The gift of growth through lessons learned
by trial and error.
The conniving conversions
and depth discussions.
Pushing each other to become better.
The intimate infatuation.
Sublime showers spent together after
romantic rendezvous.
The enchanting evenings of intimacy.
Our bodies wrapped in warmth.
Feelings of smitten with security.

LVSE.

The memories and moments traded
since we craved, cherished and enjoyed each
other's company.

Witnessing
foreshadows of a future.
A reminder,
an assurance,
a sense of confidence,
that love still exists.

All of it was a waste.
All of it.
Thank you for wasting my time.

LVSE.

LVSE.

"When I think of love, I think of the acronym L.O.V.E.

L meaning listen,

O for oath,

V for vulnerable,

E for empowering.

Whether you share love with someone or something such as a sport or instrument.

If you're able to listen, take an oath, commit, be emotionally vulnerable, open, and empower each other or oneself.

To me… that's love"

- *Joshua Brinkley*

LVSE.

I hate you

I hate you.
So don't try to convince me that
You are the love of my life.
At the end of the road
there is nothing about us that I like.
And I'm not going to lie to myself by saying
there is passion inside of us that matters.
So rest assured I will remind myself
that we are toxic, we are terrible for another
And nothing you say will make me believe
we know what love is.
No matter what happens.
We don't know love
we never met in person.
And I am in no position to believe that
Love exists in us.
Whenever I look in the mirror I always think
Are we not good together as people say?

LVSE.

Or maybe to understand us,
they need to read about our love from the bottom up.

LVSE.

<u>Meant to be</u>

When a relationship doesn't pan out,
we're so quick to think it wasn't meant to be.

What if it was…
and we simply let them slip through our fingers.

What if the reason
we blame fate for our wrongdoing,
is because we were so in love.
We were so new to it,
we didn't know what we were doing.

What if we didn't convince ourselves
it wasn't meant to be,
but it was meant to be fought for.

What if you and I were meant to part ways,
So in the end we can find each other again.

LVSE.

> What if we were
>
> better,
>
> stronger,
>
> smarter,
>
> when we found each other again.
>
> What if our only issue at this instant,
>
> was time.

LVSE.

<u>Halloqueen</u>

We met at a Halloween party.
Everyone came wearing an outfit,
and as the night went on,
you start to notice those who slowly remove
pieces of their costume.

Then I met her.

She came without a mask.
I came without a disguise.
Neither of us had a wall between us.

Without knowing,
without trying,
we had matching costumes.

LVSE.

<u>831</u>

I love you because we weren't meant to be.
We chose to be.
Destiny gave us enough reasons
to not be together.
Neither of us cared.

Whatever brought us together,
never kept us together.
That's why I love us.

LVSE.

<u>LVSE.</u>

I remember…

Being alone for the first time.
Succeeding against all odds.
Loving someone who wasn't mine.
Being loved even though I wasn't theirs.
Getting a taste of the finer things,
"one less thing."
Waiting more than a decade to kiss
the first person I had dreamt about.
Road trips with dumb and dumber.
Passing notes in a restaurant like it was high school.
Shenanigans in foreign languages,
taking hikes and flights,
from buses to planes and trains.
Starting fires with an old flame.
Staring at a navy-blue sky,
clueless of time.
Surrounded by loved ones at sea.
Feeling at home to a city you I been.

LVSE.

Flying across cities for 8-hour adventures.
Being told no so many times
the next answer was yes.
Turning a once-in-a-life time opportunity into another,
giving everything to make things work.
Getting lost as soon as you land,
using the words "you're cute" as a punchline.
Sitting by a rooftop fire in the heart of a skyline,
as you sing every melody to that pussy is mine.
Witnessing the partnerships of true love.
Matching outfits.
Dancing in a drunken brigade,
circles around an empty dancefloor.
Becoming part of a community under the sun.
Having lazy Sunday with nothing on
but the television.
Swimming to find a mermaid.
Leaving to countries with no one,
and returning with friends.

I remember…

LVSE.

<u>500 Days of Summer</u>

You remind me of summer,
I hope it never ends.
Always awaiting your arrival,
   yet always still surprised you came.
Like an alarm that's never used,
   awake before it sounds off.
You remind me of the afternoon.
Exciting, energetic, unpredictable,
   my favorite part of the day.
Warm, fresh and never the same.
You remind me of the evening.
Bright stars and shining moons.
Just bright blue skies from day until night,
              and
             you...

LVSE.

<u>No bed</u>

We don't need a bed,
 just each other.

My chest can be your pillows,
 your skin can be my covers.

LVSE.

<u>Stranger</u>

Stranger

mysterious

they instill fear and hope

and create stories of suspense

Anonymous

LVSE.

<u>Eli</u>

I loved you like a sibling.
I always pushed you to progress,
wished you nothing but success,
in your corner.
We didn't always see eye to eye,
but we always sat shoulder to shoulder.
You're now on this path
I can no longer follow.
And it's one you would rather travel solo.
I will always think of,
reminisce,
and cherish the times,
we used to be.

LVSE.

<u>My radio pt.2</u>

Your laughter is music to my ears.
The newest song to come out.
I play it,
I sing it,
over and over again in my head.
I tell everyone about it,
and tell them to listen to it.
It excites me to see,
when everyone agrees,
how good it sounds.

All I want to do,
is have the world listen to my radio.

LVSE.

<u>Love birds</u>

She gave him the nickname Noah's Ark.
She couldn't believe he was real.
He looked too much like a beautiful painting,
that belonged in a museum.
But that didn't deter him.

He explained to her,
some birds aren't meant to be caged.
Their colors are too bright
when they fly away,
together.

LVSE.

<u>Awe</u>

Why are you so beautiful to me?
Is it because during the night,
you shine your brightest?
Your big personalities in small spaces?
The way you make me feel small yet,
encouraged to reach for the stars?
Is it the way you provide me a view
on every journey?
Is it the way
you bring different people together,
no matter how different they are?
Or simply because during sleepless hours
of the evening
you're so full of life?

LVSE.

<u>Distance</u>

I can't help it,
maybe I was desperate.
I wanted to be yours,
so you were no one else's.
It happened so fast,
I went from selfish to selfless.

The moment you played music,
I became a dancer.
I never knew your sign,
but knew you'd by my cancer.
When they try to tell me,
my excuse is I understand her.
You've lied to me so many times,
I believe your answers.

So here I am,
here to stay.
I'm lost in your maze,
and I don't want to get away.

LVSE.

SVU

Oh, how he loves me,
I can't explain it.

How he yells with excitement to my face…
I know he can't help it,
he's just a loud person.

When he hits me with affection,
it's her way of playing rough.

His use of unpleasant words or name-calling,
showers me with compliments.

Our intense discussions of passion,
gives me the opportunity
to bring some fashion into my life.
Whether it's cover up or makeup,
I love to look my best.

LVSE.

But when he doesn't say a word to me,
silences feel awkward and unloving.

Whether I'm a muse or abused,
Until death does me part.

LVSE.

Hert

You say many hurtful things to me.
But I decide it's not worth to engage
in your rage.
I would rather be hurt,
if that means you will feel better.

LVSE.

<u>Arms</u>

When you brush up from behind,
and wrap your arms around me.
All the troubles of the world around me
slowly fade away.

LVSE.

LVSE.

"I'd rather have loyalty than love
cause love really don't mean jack.
See, love is just a feeling.
You can love somebody and still stab them in the back.
It don't take much to love.
You can love somebody just by being attached.
See, loyalty is an action.
You can love or hate me and still have my back"

- *Shéyaa Bin Abraham-Joseph*

LVSE.

<u>**Amnesia**</u>

He tries so hard not to get excited,
not get his hopes up.
That the best defense is offense.
If no expectations exist,
no disappointments can occur.

Then she laughs,
amnesia strikes,
and he is back at square one.

LVSE.

My type of wine

The honeymoon phase,
what an incredible taste.
The flavor that keeps giving.
What if we were to bottle all of those emotions and feelings into our very own wine.

We harvest our wants and desires
while they are at the stages of immaturity.
Press each other for intimate details of another
from the periods of mystery.
Ferment our chemistry of infatuation while
clarifying each other's intentions with flirtatious smirks and remarks.
And finally,
age our love that withstood trials and tribulations.

We would only drink when we're older,
when our fire starts to burn out.
But as we aged, our love has aged,
beautifully over time.

LVSE.

More wise, smooth, and precise with more flavor.

Once our special bottle of wine is opened, sparks will fly.

Middle

If I could be anywhere,
in the entire country,
in the entire world,
or in the entire universe
for a vacation,

I would be in you.

I would turn this bed into a resort,
the Cayman islands,
or whatever your heart desired,
to stay in the middle of your love.

LVSE.

Sometimes

Sometimes,
I open my eyes when we kiss
so I know this isn't a dream
and it's really you.

LVSE.

<u>You're*</u>

You're haunting when I daydream.
So many things you complained about.
All the sacrifices you wouldn't do.
Your illogical hypocritical stances,
your attitude.

But to be honest,
before I resume back to real life,
an ounce of me wishes we still worked out.

LVSE.

<u>Sedona</u>

He took us to the moist desert of Sedona,
where sunsets wrestle on top of one another.
When the sun came down,
I couldn't tell where heaven stopped
and when earth began.

LVSE.

<u>Poison</u>

She was a smart girl,

she knew better.

She believed in Shakespeare

but knew Romeo and Juliet were not role models.

She wasn't looking to be a rebound,

too wise to be naïve.

When the time came,

and she found love,

she picked her poison.

The poison that would keep her love alive.

LVSE.

__In a blink__

It's been a few months since you moved away.
We rarely speak anymore
and I never get to see you.

So, when I ran into you last night,
though unannounced,
it was a pleasant surprise.

It was just like the old times.
We spoke,
we danced,
told lies,
held hands.
We flirted,
we kissed,
told each other what we missed.

LVSE.

And in a blink of both eyes,
you were no longer there.

Now I am in your twisted reality
where the best part of my day,
is when I go to sleep.

Last night I had a dream about you,
and I never wanted to wake up.

LVSE.

Easy to water

It's amazing how you have a hold on me.
I sit alone in the desert,
waiting for you,
waiting for your love to rain on me.
Long periods go by,
and no attention is given.
The minute you give me water,
my thirst becomes quenched,
and I continue living on the bare minimum.

Our love may grow slowly,
just know my sharp spikes aren't meant for you,
but to protect us.

It's as if,
I was made dying for your love.

LVSE.

<u>Shapes</u>

She always finds herself in familiar waters.
Waist deep,
swimming in circles when he's around.

He is no different.

When she is up and about,
he finds himself excited
not knowing which way is up or down.

LVSE.

<u>Memories</u>

Memories…

The only invention created that allows us to travel through time.

The only innovation that captures time and changes it simultaneously.

The ability to re-live the past,

experience the feelings we once had,

and remove us from the presence of the present.

However…

Every moment a day decides to go for a drive,

a memory is lost unknowingly.

Like missing car keys,

you never realize they are misplaced until you try to recall where they are.

LVSE.

> Or a picture with missing details,
> becoming abstract art.

> As much as I love to travel through time,
> time continuously eludes us.

> So it's just my partner and I,
> creating new destinations for time travel.

LVSE.

LVSE.

"Love is a choice. Love is moments of profound rejoice. Love is I have found the perfection in the imperfection."

- *Melisa Collazo*

LVSE.

<u>Faith</u>

I have faith.
Not that we will end up together,
but one day,
one day you will attend class,
you will do the math,
you will pay attention,
to the lesson,
and learn
all of the surprises, all of the gifts,
all the sacrifices, all of the rifts,
and all the time spent equaled love.

I have faith that when you learn,
it will be too late
and you'll never admit the mistake,
of walking away.

We should

We should kiss.
Not because you noticed me
when I walked in the room.
But because you decided I was worth
getting to know.
And I haven't stopped thinking about you
since.

LVSE.

<u>Sun-kissed</u>

When you grab my face,
and stare into my eyes.
I feel like I've been sun-kissed
during a cold winter day by the sky.

LVSE.

<u>Freely</u>

My heart was never stolen.
Everything I have,
I freely gave to you
without you ever having to ask.

LVSE.

<u>Red-handed</u>

I caught you staring at me
and you wanted to be caught.
But so did I.

Jossie

Carnivores, your eye lashes are,
searching for weak targets.
To convince prey like myself,
to not be scared by your
big bright beautiful beady eyes.
But to dive in your deep pools of desire,
that reflect glistening waters of lust.

When I stare into your eyes,
an opalescent shade of vibrant colors,
I become hypnotized.
Fear turns into lust,
and lust turn to love.
I am no longer scared that I can't swim,
I hope that I will drown.

LVSE.

<u>Brighter days</u>

Colors appear brighter.
Food has more flavor.
The air we breathe tastes more fresh.
Puzzles are easy to piece.
My shoulders feel lighter.
I suddenly look more attractive in every image I see.

All news is good news ever since I've met you.

LVSE.

<u>Scent</u>

Your scent,
heaven sent,
makes me lose my common sense.
I could write journals and letters,
with everything I let her,
get away with.
She has rode me
down roads,
where cars aren't allowed,
only moans aloud.
She never had brakes we could use,
and never asked for a break.
When it starts to mist,
showers with her I can't miss.
There's nothing in this world you could buy here,
that could convince me it's time to hear bye.

LVSE.

<u>Yoda</u>

Hatred
frigid, cold,
unmoving, dry, icy,
melting, slushy, slippery, wet,
dripping, damp, humid,
warm, cozy
Love.

LVSE.

<u>Shelved</u>

I've been taken off the shelf,
where so many other books rest,
to collect dust.
They would rather avoid the opportunity,
to be taken and returned to the community,
and no longer discussed.

At this moment you chose me,
I am open to read,
for your eyes only.
When you hold me,
grab the back of my spine,
and read between every line,
my story feels it found it's reason for time.
I just want you stay long enough,
to turn the page.

LVSE.

<u>Heartbreak</u>

A broken clock may be right twice a day,
and twice a day a broken heart
may need to write hope and faith.

Just like the clock
it's not meant to be
broken forever.

LVSE.

<u>Wants</u>

She wants to see
chains dangling in front of her face.

He wants a
reason to do laundry.

LVSE.

<u>Long drives</u>

I love sitting in the passenger seat
when he drives.
I get to look out the window
to see the gorgeous world God created,
and a beautiful man He created,
for me.

LVSE.

<u>Radiance</u>

Your personality is radiant by design.
Whichever room it is
becomes appealing
the moment you walk in.
I can't put my finger on it,
but my God,
I love it.

It's clear your beauty within
outshines everything else.

LVSE.

<u>Stop</u>

It's been on my mind,
I made the decision about an hour ago.

I don't mean to be rude,
but please stop talking and kiss me.

LVSE.

<u>Makes me feel</u>

The way he grabs me by the hands

when I'm in need,

makes the air I breathe,

blissful,

when I am being choked…

The way she wraps her legs around me

when I enter the hidden temple,

makes me feel safe,

when I am being trapped…

LVSE.

<u>Life</u>

Love
imitates life.
Always moving, evolving continuously.
Never-ending adventures with highs and lows.
Lifted and sinking stomachs,
swaying gracefully.
Rollercoasters of emotions
with laugh fulfilled journeys.
Change of seasons,
Reflecting,
mirrored colors.
-reflect-
colors mirrored
reflecting,
seasons of change.
journeys fulfilled laugh with
emotions of rollercoasters.
Gracefully swaying
stomachs sinking and lifted

LVSE.

Lows and highs with adventures ending-never.
Continuously evolving, moving always,
life imitates
Love.

LVSE.

LVSE.

About the author

E.J. Tiago is a writer from Albany, NY currently living in Chicago. All types of art, including writing and photography, have been his passion from a young age. All works of art from poetry to paintings are created by him. Tiago has always felt the need to create as purely as possible by transforming blank pages into a canvas of thought.

E.J. Tiago's library of poetry includes:

PlayBoy Diary

11 Missed Calls

Directions From A Lost Compass

For more information and updates:

www.amazon.com/author/ejtiago

Instagram: @FiveOneEight_Studio

Instagram: @518z_VeryOwn

LVSE.

LVSE.

<u>Molly pt.2</u>

You speak to me as if you know me.
I hear you digging
for deep rooted insecurities.
Telling a story of one who is lost,
yet,
seeking a path towards attention.
Explaining the view of a glasshouse
is better on the outside than inside.

I try to understand your thoughts of dismay.
But I notice you are looking at the mirror,
with all of these words you say.

Made in the USA
Coppell, TX
27 February 2024